Counting Stars

Counting Stars

INSPIRING DEVOTIONALS FOR FAMILIES

William L. Coleman

BETHANY HOUSE PUBLISHERS
Minneapolis, Minnesota 55438
A Division of Bethany Fellowship, Inc.

Counting Stars
by William L. Coleman

Scripture portions are taken from The Living Bible,
copyright © 1971 by Tyndale House Publishers, Wheaton, Ill.
Used by permission.

Photos by John Billman, Dick Easterday, Rita Eltgroth,
Loren Garborg, Fred Renich, John Thornberg and Roger Werth.

Published by Bethany House Publishers
A division of Bethany Fellowship, Inc.
6820 Auto Club Road, Minneapolis, MN 55438

Printed in the United States of America

Library of Congress Cataloging in Publication Data

Coleman, William L.
   Counting stars.

   SUMMARY: Links Scripture, scientific information about nature,
and a meditative thought regarding the wonders of God in nature.
   I. Title.
BV4870.C63   242'.6'2   76-28973
ISBN 0-87123-055-0

Dedicated to
Mary, Jim, June

Devotionals for families with young children
by William L. Coleman

Counting Stars, meditations on God's creation.

My Magnificent Machine, devotionals centered around the marvels of the human body.

Listen to the Animals, lessons from the animal world.

On Your Mark, challenges from the lives of well-known athletes.

The Good Night Book, bedtime inspirationals (especially for those who may be afraid of the dark).

More About My Magnificent Machine, more devotionals describing parts of the human body and how they reflect the genius of the Creator.

Today I feel Like a Warm Fuzzy, devotionals for small children which help them to identify and learn how to respond to their own feelings and emotions.

Singing Penguins and Puffed-Up Toads, devotionals about creatures of the sea.

About the Author

WILLIAM L. COLEMAN is a graduate of the Washington Bible College in Washington, D.C., and Grace Theological Seminary in Winona Lake, Indiana.

He has pastored three churches: a Baptist church in Michigan, a Mennonite church in Kansas and an Evangelical Free Church in Aurora, Nebraska. He is a Staley Foundation lecturer.

The author of 75 magazine articles, his by-line has appeared in *Christianity Today, Eternity, Good News Broadcaster, Campus Life, Moody Monthly, Evangelical Beacon,* and *The Christian Reader.*

Coleman has written eight children's devotional books.

Contents

A Look Around

The Bible is packed with good illustrations from nature. Jesus Christ often talked about the world around Him because there were great lessons to be learned from the wind, the animals and the flowers.

Today God is still teaching us through the elements. We could appreciate both God and nature more by listening well.

The following chapters are a look at the Scriptures, and explain why the writers referred to certain parts of nature.

Read, appreciate, enjoy, marvel at the wonderful world God has made.

William L. Coleman
Aurora, Nebraska

one

Counting Stars

On some clear night, go outside and look at the beautiful sky. If all the conditions are right, you can count 2,000 stars out in space.

You might think that is all the stars there are if it weren't for an Italian professor named Galileo Galilei. In 1609 Galileo was the first person to ever look at the skies through a telescope. He saw moons around Jupiter, craters on the moon and thousands of stars that make up the Milky Way. Though people had studied the stars for many years, now they could see wonders they had not dreamed of before.

One of the things that telescopes have allowed us to discover is that the earth is part of a huge galaxy filled with at least 100,000 stars. Then also it has been discovered that there are one million known galaxies, and we do not know how many we cannot see. By simple arithmetic we can figure out that there are over 100 billion stars which we can see by telescope.

The final information on all of the stars and all of the galaxies is not yet in the hands of the scientists. However, these statistics have long been in the hands of God. God has always known how many stars there are and He is able to count them. But the writer of the Psalms goes further than that. He reminds us that God has named and accounted for every single star.

An astronomer who works at the Hayden Planetarium in New York claims that he has never met a professional astronomer who is an atheist. After studying the vast beauty of space they must believe in a Great Designer.

1. Who was the first person to use a telescope?
2. How many galaxies are in the universe?
3. Do you talk to God when you are sad? When you are happy?

He counts the stars and calls them all by name.—Psalm 147:4

two

Rainbows Have a Purpose

There are certain signs in the sky which allow us to be amateur weathermen. One of these signs is the rainbow.

The sun makes the beautiful arc across the sky by reflecting its rays through a curtain of falling rain. When we stand in the correct position, facing away from the sun, we can see the radiant colors.

By watching the rainbow we can know if a rain shower is coming toward us or going away. If we see the bow to the east at the end of the day, we know the shower or storm has passed. If, however, we see the rainbow to the west at the beginning of the day, we know that the storm is still coming. A rainbow must have rain and its position will tell us whether the rain is coming or going.

A lot of people joke about searching for the pot of gold at the end of the rainbow, but that is just a legend and not worth the search.

Many years ago, after God had allowed the earth to be flooded during Noah's time, God made us a promise. He said that He would never again flood the entire earth. Then, just so we would not forget, He put a special sign in the sky. It is made up of beautiful colors and we call it a rainbow. It serves as a sign of two things: one, to tell the weather; and, two, to remind us of God's promise.

The Bible makes a lot of promises from God to His people. Every time we see the rainbow we can remember that God has kept that promise and He will keep all the rest of them.

15

1. How are rainbows made?
2. What does a rainbow in the east at evening mean?
3. Name one thing you would like God to give you.

I have placed my rainbow in the clouds as a sign of my promise until the end of time, to you and to all the earth.—Genesis 9:13

three

Lightning Is Frightening

Why would God, the Great Designer, give the world something as useless and as frightening as lightning? It sets forest fires, damages electric wires and does a lot of other destruction.

While it is true that lightning sends a lot of children (and even some adults) scrambling under their beds, don't dismiss this giant from the sky as merely useless. This loud, dramatic noise plays a major part in feeding the plants in this world—in fact, so much so that plants could not live without it.

Eighty percent of our atmosphere is made up of nitrogen which is essential to vegetation. God devised a beautiful plan to take the nitrogen out of the air, change it into food and get it to the plants. When lightning rattles through the sky, its intense heat dissolves the nitrogen into the rain which carries it to earth.

After a severe storm you can smell the acid in the air. That smell is the fertilizer which God sent down for the plants. And He starts the process with a seemingly useless racket we call lightning.

Our God is not a voiceless spirit who cannot think. Our world is not an accident made up of strange little parts which fell together. God had a plan and a purpose for everything He put into it.

God also has a clear, definite purpose for you, for me and for everyone else. God explained that purpose in Colossians 1:16. He said we were created by Jesus Christ and "for him." We find our highest purpose in life by living for Jesus Christ.

1. Name one purpose of lightning.
2. What is the strange odor after a rainstorm?
3. Name one purpose God has for you.

It is his voice that echoes in the thunder of the storm clouds. He causes mist to rise upon the earth; he sends the lightning and brings the rain, and from his treasures he brings the wind.—Jeremiah 10:13

four

Ambitious Ants

Ants must be the hardest working insects in the world. An ant can carry 52 times its own weight. That would be the same as an 80-pound boy lifting 4,160 pounds in one package.

Ants are sociable creatures and live in colonies rather than alone. Some ant "cities" have as few as 12 or as many as 240,000 ants living together. There are thousands of species of ants. A survey in Maryland found over one billion ants of one species per acre. As you can see, the total number of ants would be uncountable.

One species of ant is the harvester which collects large pieces of grain to store for the winter. Their underground nests are divided into nurseries, granaries or fungus gardens. On sunny days they rake moist grain outside and let it dry off to keep it from sprouting.

As the writer of Proverbs tells us, the harvester ant has no king to tell it what to do. They have a queen, but she is not the boss. Without anyone nagging them, the ants faithfully go about their jobs. They know work has to be done.

We are sociable creatures just as the ant. We enjoy life best when we pitch in and do our part. Whether it is at school, on a job or at home, laziness hurts instead of helps.

1. How strong are ants?
2. How large are ant cities?
3. What is your favorite job?

Take a lesson from the ants, you lazy fellow. Learn from their ways and be wise! For though they have no king to make them work, yet they labor hard all summer, gathering food for the winter.—Proverbs 6:6-8

five

Gone Like the Wind

All of us live at the bottom of a 20-mile-deep ocean. Fortunately for us it is not an ocean of water but rather a sea of air.

That air keeps getting disturbed continuously. Sometimes it is agitated slowly and other times very briskly or even violently. As it begins to move noticeably, air then becomes wind.

There are two actions which cause wind to move. One, the warm air of the hot tropics mixes with the cold air of the polar areas. When they meet they start to move. The second action is the earth's rotation at the equator. The rotation of the earth can reach 1,000 miles per hour there, and that makes wind.

In Palestine the south winds could be gentle but also very hot. Luke 12:55 states, "When the south wind blows you say, 'Today will be a scorcher.' And it is." They could also get cool, rainy winds from the north (Prov. 25:23), particularly in March.

Just as on the plains of Kansas, the people of Palestine also know how to live in wind. It blows often and can easily carry things away. In Iran the windy season is long and the winds are capable of carrying enough sand to cover an entire village. God wants to remind us that life is short even for the youngest of us. Soon we will be gone just like a leaf carried in the wind.

Most of us think we will live a very long time. But time passes quickly and soon life has blown away. While

we are young we need to serve Jesus Christ before we move on quickly.

1. What causes wind?
2. When does Palestine get cool winds?
3. When is it a good time to follow Christ?

He is like a father to us, tender and sympathetic to those who reverence him. For he knows we are but dust, and that our days are few and brief, like grass, like flowers, blown by the wind and gone forever.—Psalm 103:13-16

six

The Stinging Scorpion

Some of nature's creatures have such terrible reputations that just the mention of their name gives people the creeps. To know about a scorpion is to distrust and dislike him.

A missionary to Mexico once said, "You learn to live with scorpions. If you have left a newspaper lying around for an hour, you always smash it before picking it up. There is probably a scorpion in it."

Scorpions look a little bit like a lobster and some of them do live in the water; however, the majority of them live in hot, dry climates all over the world. Most of them are only two or three inches long and they have a long tail that swings back and forth. Many of the species have a stinger on the end of their tail, and they can poison an insect before they eat it, or they can make a human being very sick.

Technically speaking, scorpions are not insects but arachnids and are air-breathing invertebrates. They belong to the same family as spiders, mites and ticks, and they have four legs.

When Jesus wanted to teach His disciples about prayer, He used an illustration that everyone in a hot climate would understand. If your son asks you for something nice like an egg (or food), would you give him a scorpion that would sting him and make him sick? Well, God is the greatest Father of them all and He is looking for good things to give us. He is not trying to make life miserable for us.

1. What do scorpions look like?
2. Where is a scorpion stinger?
3. Name two things God has given you.

You men who are fathers — if your boy asks for bread, do you give him a stone? If he asks for a fish, do you give him a snake? If he asks for an egg, do you give him a scorpion? (Of course not!)—Luke 11:11, 12

seven

Leaping Locusts

Many of us are more familiar with the grasshopper than with its relative, the locust. They look something alike and have several similar habits and very often are confused for each other.

The locust would probably be overlooked as just another insect except for its peculiar ability to gather in large groups and swarm across the countryside, eating and destroying practically all of the vegetation. Some of these winged hoppers can move as far as 1,240 miles away from their place of origin.

Normally there are sufficient enemies of the locust that help kill them off and keep them from becoming too numerous. However, when nature gets out of balance the locusts can start to move and practically nothing can stand in their way. They can climb walls, rocks, hills and cross trenches, often marching over each other's bodies. In 1932 they were reported to have crossed the Suez Canal.

In recent years special organizations have been formed to help keep the number of locusts in check.

Under normal conditions God seems to allow nature to take its course. He hung the stars in space and circled the earth with life-giving air. There are some times when the forces of nature naturally become over-stocked and there are floods or plagues of locusts. But once in a while during the thousands of years of history God has specifically caused nature to bring catastrophe.

God holds the future of all nations in His hands. If those nations prefer godlessness and refuse to obey Him, God might decide to send tragedy. Maybe armies will attack them, floods overwhelm them or locusts strip them. By some means, either love or force, He wants our nation to follow God and not Satan.

1. What do locusts eat?
2. What canal have locust crossed?
3. If something bad happens, do you feel closer to God or not? Why?

If I shut up the heavens so that there is no rain, or if I command the locust swarms to eat up all of your crops, or if I send an epidemic among you. . . .—2 Chronicles 7:13

eight

Webs Won't Work

All of us have seen cobwebs around our house—maybe in the basement or even upstairs where we live. Originally these were spider webs, but now they have become tangled and caked with dust and dirt. Spider webs are common because there are so many of those eight-legged little animals (they are not insects) who spin silk and stretch it from corner to corner.

To us the web is merely a curious nuisance, a sticky thread that we might walk into once in a while. But to the spider these silk strings are a way of life. They use them for everything from hunting to housing.

If a spider is in trouble he can escape by sliding down a silk thread, called a dragline, on which he lowers rapidly to the ground or floor. He can use the same line to pounce quickly on an enemy or jump on some food.

When in the market for a new home he might take that same silk and wrap up a leaf, designing a nest for himself and his family. He can use the webbing to encircle his eggs and give them a soft resting place.

Nevertheless, the most famous use of the web is to spread a net in a corner or across an opening and wait for an unsuspecting fly or other insect. One bite of his fangs will kill the trapped victim, and there is his dinner.

Webs work very well for spiders. They are thin enough to fool insects and yet strong enough to do their job. However, they are not quite strong enough to hold a human being. The man Job had all of the good things in life. He had money, houses, cattle, employees, a large family—and then he lost practically everything he owned, including his children.

After his tragedies he was able to offer some advice to all of us. We need to trust God to take care of us. If we say, "Someday I will be rich and famous and then I will be safe and happy," it will be like leaning on spider webs, and they will not hold us up.

But if we trust in God, we will always be able to depend on Him because He never will "collapse."

1. What is a dragline?
2. Where do spiders put their webs?
3. Why is it better to trust God than to trust riches?

A man without God is trusting in a spider's web. Everything he counts on will collapse.—Job 8:14

nine

Guns and Snails

The one who wrote this Psalm must have spent his childhood loving nature. It is easy to picture him lying on his stomach out on the grass watching a small, slow snail crawl around on the plants. Usually you have to get flat on the ground to see them, because some snails are as small as pin heads. Other species are as large as two feet long.

The technical name for this little land friend is gastropod, which simply means belly and foot since they crawl on their bellies. The snails that live on land usually try to find damp places to stay because heat tends to dry them up. They live off the plants and have thousands of tiny weak teeth. Instead of male and female snails, each land variety is both a male and a female all in one.

One of the snail's protective devices is a tricky system. You will notice that snails often leave a wet trail behind them as they walk. This trail is a sticky substance called mucus, and many times their enemies, ants and beetles, get stuck in this "glue" while going after one of them.

While the young lad who wrote Psalm 58 watched snails, he learned something else about them which he included in verse 8. When land snails die they do not leave fossils in rock as many other living creatures. Their shell has no aragonite and so they merely dissolve. The writer applied this fact to life and he said that he hoped his enemies' weapons would just dissolve like the snail who melts away.

People have always been at war in one way or another and yet God does not want us to hate and fight. Jesus taught, "Love your enemies" and "Blessed is

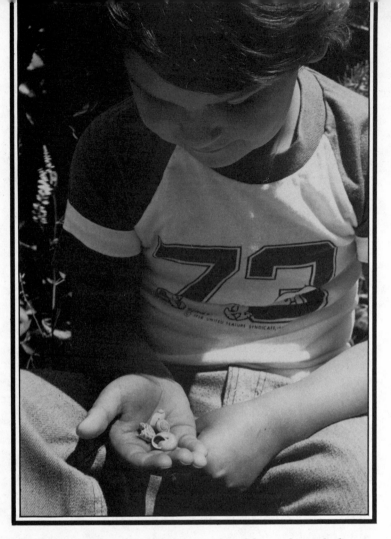

the peacemaker." Christians should work to help enemies become friends and let their weapons of destruction simply dissolve like the snail in the rock.

1. What is the technical name for snails?
2. What is mucus?
3. Is it hard to love your enemies? Explain.

Let them be as snails that dissolve into slime; and as those who die at birth, who never see the sun.—Psalm 58:8

As Fresh as the Dew

When we are very young we learn what dew is because we walk in the grass without shoes and our feet get wet very quickly. But have we ever considered how the dew got there and what it does?

A good clear night is the best time for dew to form because then the objects on the ground, blades of grass, leaves, etc., cool off best. As they cool down, the night air touches the cold objects and forms little particles of water. We call this process condensation.

If the ground temperature gets too cold (below freezing), the dew becomes frost.

In areas where the rainfall is good, dew still helps

31

the growing plants somewhat; but in dry or tropical areas the dew is a tremendous benefit. In some desert areas the plants are dependent on dew for long periods of time.

Palestine needs dew because parts of the land are almost totally rainless for four summer months, and the days are very hot. Cool winds from the Mediterranean help increase the dew, but the hot winds from the desert keep the land dry and are disastrous if they continue for a long time.

The writer of this Psalm is talking about Jesus Christ (see Matt. 22:41-45), and he is listing some of the difficulties He would face. His job would be hard because He would have to face many enemies in His task. But the writer tells Him to be filled with courage because God will give Him strength every day just as the morning dew settles and refreshes the plants on the ground.

Life is filled with jobs that you and I do not want to do, and yet we have to do them. (Even Jesus Christ faced these.) We have to do them because our parents, our teachers, our friends or our God tell us to do them. And sometimes we do hard jobs just because we know it is the right thing to do. On those tough days, doing those hard jobs, God gives us a promise. He will give us strength each day in the same way that dew gives strength to a hot, thirsty ground.

1. What causes dew?
2. How is frost made?
3. How can God help us do a job we don't want to do?

And your strength shall be renewed day by day like morning dew.—Psalm 110:3

Collecting Tears

People always have tears in their eyes whether they are crying or not. These tears play a vital role in maintaining one of the most finely balanced parts of the human body.

Normally we think of tears as those drops of water which come out of the eye when we cry. However, the liquid which constantly surrounds the eye comes from our tear duct. This water serves as a lubricant to keep the eye moving smoothly and as a cleanser to carry dust particles or hair away from the cornea. If a person's eye would ever lose its fluid, he would go blind.

Tears come from tiny ducts which are located under the eyelid. God placed a special opening in the nose in case the tear ducts produced too much liquid. This explains why the nose often runs when a person cries.

A number of things cause an individual to cry: irritants such as onion vapor or smoke, or natural elements such as bright light or wind can activate the ducts. Continuous movements of the eyelids may also increase the flow.

Our bodies are so marvelously made that strong emotions will affect our tear balance. All tears are not sad. A great deal of happiness or laughter will cause our eyes to "water." Likewise, strong sadness will make the ducts produce faster than the eye or valve in the nose can handle it, and the result is an overflow which runs down our cheeks.

Some people are embarrassed to cry and often we are discouraged from crying; however, a good healthy use of the tear ducts is a very natural process.

Most of the time we take tears very much for granted. They are no big deal; they are usually there when we need them and sometimes they betray how we really feel. The author of Psalm 56 sometimes couldn't sleep at night, and more than once he found himself crying in his bed. Yet he felt so strongly that God cared about each thing in his life that he even imagined God collecting each tear and putting it into a bottle. He could picture God keeping a record of his tears in a special book.

Indeed, God cares about our tears because He cares about what makes us cry. God couldn't be much more personal or loving than that.

1. Where do tears come from?
2. What causes tears?
3. What does it mean that God puts our tears in bottles?

You have seen me tossing and turning through the night. You have collected all my tears and preserved them in your bottle! You have recorded every one in your book.—Psalm 56:8

twelve

What Is Under the Sea?

Seventy percent of the earth is covered by water and people have always been fascinated by what goes on under the sea. However, until recently man has learned only a little about the ocean because of its immense size.

To get some idea of its depth, compare the ocean with the largest mountain on earth, Mt. Everest. It is almost 30,000 feet high, and yet if it were placed in certain parts of the ocean it would simply disappear without a trace. The Hawaiian Islands are the top of an ocean mountain 36,000 feet high. At this point alone the sea is over seven miles deep.

During our lifetime some of the most exciting studies ever done are being performed by scientists under the ocean (called oceanography). Some scientists believe that man can live under the ocean, and they have established "colonies" where men have lived for weeks without surfacing. Other people are farming the ocean. In the Gulf of Taranto, Italy, shellfish are being grown under certain controls, and their annual production is 11,000 pounds of meat per acre.

The number and variety of fish, plants, insects and microscopic creatures is so enormous that one is reluctant to even guess. Of the arthropods alone (joint-legged creatures) there are 35,000 different types. Everyone has heard of the starfish, but how many of us realize that there are 2,000 varieties of starfish?

The seas contain unseen wonders and are packed

with unimagined possibilities. A number of today's youth will grow up to become oceanography scientists.

When Paul and Barnabas preached at Lystra the crowd was so amazed at the sermons that they yelled, "These men are gods in human bodies." They wanted to worship the ones who brought the message.

Quickly Paul corrected them. Only one person is worth worshipping. The living God who made the 3,000-pound manta and the beautiful clown sea slugs is the real God. The rich variety under the ocean reminds us how remarkable God is.

1. How deep is the ocean?
2. How many varieties of starfish are in the sea?
3. What are some of the things we sometimes make our gods?

Men! What are you doing? We are merely human beings like yourselves! We have come to bring you the Good News that you are invited to turn from the worshipping of these foolish things and to pray instead to the living God who made heaven and earth and seas and everything in them.—Acts 14:15

thirteen

The King Who Loved Nature

Often some of the busiest people in the world find time to pursue a good hobby. President Roosevelt collected stamps and President Eisenhower played golf. King Solomon made time in his busy schedule to become an authority on nature.

Some historians say Solomon had a beautiful cinnamon garden. It's easy to picture the famous king checking the bark on these valuable trees. The bark would later be used to make perfume to offer to the woman of his heart.

One wonders if the king spent hours watching the harvester ant gather grain. Later Solomon wrote of how good a worker this ant was.

Maybe he studied the dangerous carpet snake and

tried to make medicine to fight its poisonous bite. Can we picture him flat on his stomach in the mud watching little creatures swimming around and trying to figure out where they came from?

How often did Solomon watch the ostrich and scratch his head? Though the ostrich doesn't really stick its head in the sand, it does so many other ridiculous things that it may qualify as one of nature's dumbest creatures. For example, the ostrich can run fast but since it runs against the wind enemies can easily follow and kill it. The ostrich buries its eggs in the sand but often leaves a few showing and they are easily stolen. If danger comes the ostrich will abandon its chicks or eggs and run for its life. Their feathers make lovely fans.

Solomon enjoyed watching nature. He planted gardens and brought trees and animals, such as the peacock, into Israel. By studying nature Solomon learned a lot about people and about God. Many of the things he learned he wrote down into proverbs or shared in his courts.

Years later Paul wrote, "Since earliest times men have seen the earth and the sky and all God made, and have known of his existence and great eternal power" (Rom. 1:20).

1. What was Solomon's hobby?
2. What does an ostrich do that is foolish?
3. How does nature point to God?

He was a great naturalist, with interest in animals, birds, snakes, fish and trees—the great cedars of Lebanon down to the tiny hyssop which grows in cracks in the wall. And kings from many lands sent their ambassadors to him for advice.—1 Kings 4:33, 34

fourteen

Fifteen-Pound Tail

Some of us have probably never seen a live sheep except in a zoo. And a good many of us have never eaten sheep (called lamb). However, in Palestine sheep were one of the most important animals around and every person had seen them.

Sheep, and their close relative the ram, are mentioned 500 times in the Bible. They were kept as farm animals as early as Genesis chapter four, so they have been important for a long time.

During the time of Jesus the most usual type of sheep was an odd looking animal called the broad-tailed sheep. They are raised in Israel today, and their tail might weigh anywhere from 10 to 15 pounds. People liked to eat the tail because it was considered the best part of the animal.

Not everyone agrees on whether or not sheep are really so important, but the people during biblical times were glad to have them. They supplied good food to eat, wool for clothing and even good milk for breakfast. If someone needed a home, he would use their hides to make a strong tent; if anyone needed to buy something, he used sheep for money; and if he wanted to play his favorite song, he merely picked up a sheep horn and made sweet music.

Sheep were so important that God gave special laws to protect them from being mistreated. They even got one day off each week just like the human beings. There were a lot of shepherds in Israel to help raise this much-needed animal.

Since sheep were so valuable and useful, they were watched carefully by the person who owned and cared for them. He often slept with his sheep in the field and knew if anything happened to them. Sometimes wolves or even people might try to steal them.

If a shepherd woke up one morning and noticed that one sheep had gotten lost in the night, he would move quickly to find it. He might put the rest of the sheep in a pen and then go out and search all day until he found that lost sheep.

1. How much do sheep tails weigh in Palestine?
2. How were sheep hides used?
3. How is Jesus our shepherd?

This was his answer: "If you had just one sheep, and it fell into a well on the Sabbath, would you work to rescue it that day? Of course you would."—Matthew 12:11

fifteen

What Good Are Volcanoes?

Photo © Roger Werth, *Daily News*, Longview, W.A.

There may be more active volcanoes in the world than most of us realize. There are approximately 500 active, fire-shooting volcanoes, and many of them are located in the area of the Pacific Ocean.

Most of us look at volcanoes as huge furnaces which throw out tons of fire and cause enormous damage. There is certainly a lot of truth to this. In 1815, 47,000 people died near Java after an eruption. One of the world's worst destruction of life by a volcano occurred at St. Pierre in the West Indies. At that time 30,000 people were killed. One man lived because he was a prisoner in a thick-walled jail.

Despite its well-known horrors these explosions play an important role in our survival. The most obvious benefits come from the gases which pour out. The gases send out nitrogen, hydrogen and carbon dioxide. These substances feed plants which in turn produce oxygen which helps people breathe.

The lava which pours from these mountains creates excellent farm soil. Consequently, many people prefer to live close to a volcano.

Volcano energy is being used to modern advantage in many countries. It is converted into electric energy in Italy, laundry steam in New Zealand, and steam heat in Iceland. This is called geothermal energy.

All volcanoes shoot out gas in the form of steam, which may be as hot as 1,000 degrees F.

There are two major factors in causing a volcano to erupt. Below the surface the earth often shifts. This shifting rock creates friction which naturally makes heat. This adds to the hot melted rock and gas which is trying to rise. The result is an explosion which the earth needs to keep its balance.

Why would God put such violent mountains on the earth? They are not intended to hurt man but to help him and keep the earth safe. A raging volcano, then, is not the wrath of God but an evidence of His goodness.

A volcano is a call to worship. When it shoots its lava, rock, gas and flame, we can all thank God that He created a beautiful earth which takes care of itself with such splendor.

1. How many active volcanoes are there?
2. How is lava helpful?
3. Why did God create volcanoes?

Praise God forever! How he must rejoice in all his work! The earth trembles at his glance; the mountains burst into flame at his touch.—Psalm 104:31, 32

sixteen

An Old Health Food

Have you ever been playing ball on a very hot day, and as the perspiration poured down your face a drop ran onto your tongue? Maybe you remember it as tasting a bit salty. That is exactly what it was, since our perspiration, blood and tears all contain salt.

That small container of salt which we see daily on our table and take for granted is actually one of the most important substances in the world. It consists of sodium and chlorine and is absolutely essential to good health.

But then, there are thousands of practical uses for salt, some of which might really surprise us. Salt can be used to build highways, to melt ice, to make ice cream, to purify water, to preserve hay, to make soap and even to mix in water and use as a mouthwash.

Fortunately for all of us there is much salt available in the world. Salt can be taken out of the sea, mined out of the earth, and even dug out of wells as we would oil. The United States produces more salt than any other country, with China following at a distant second.

At one time workers were paid in salt instead of money. Consequently the word salary originally came from salt.

During the life of Christ salt played a very important role. One major use for salt was to keep things from spoiling. Since there were no refrigerators or freezers, people rubbed salt into their meat. If it was prepared correctly the meat could be kept from rotting for long periods of time.

A second use of salt was, as today, to season food. Some terrible tasting meals could be enriched with just a little tang from the salt jar. This also helped keep the body balanced by supplying the portion needed by the blood and cells.

Jesus compared salt with people. Good people help the world around them from becoming spoiled and rotten. If people didn't stand up for the good and godly things in life, then the selfish, cruel, and mean ones would rule everything.

However, if the good people, the followers of Christ, also start to act mean and hateful, then they can no longer help by being the salt of the earth.

1. What is in salt?
2. Where can you find salt?
3. How does Jesus want us to be salt?

What good is salt that has lost its saltiness? Flavorless salt is fit for nothing — not even fertilizer. It is worthless and must be thrown out. Listen well, if you would understand my meaning.—Luke 14:34, 35

seventeen

The Long Bear Sleep

What do we think of when we hear "Teddy Bear"? Maybe our mind pictures a peaceful, cuddly, soft doll resting quietly on a bed. Actually a real bear is very much like the toy variety and it would like to be just as friendly.

If bears had their way, they would live at peace with everyone. Most bears don't like to fight and if possible will walk away from any danger. They don't have many enemies, mostly just a few other bears and some people. They even walk into campsites looking for food because they are easygoing and don't expect trouble.

However, when bears sense danger, they can be as mean as any animal in nature. They get angry very quickly and can erupt into killers in a second. Because they are unpredictable, people do well to treat them cautiously and keep their distance.

Not known as great workers, bears like to take long naps which last for the entire winter. Technically speaking, bears do not hibernate; they only sleep. They may wake up on a cold, snowy day, take a walk and come back to continue the long nap.

As winter begins the bear increases its eating considerably. It is trying to gain fat to live off while it sleeps. The bear then looks for a snug cave, hollow log or even thick brush where it can sleep. Just how they know when to go to bed is uncertain, but somehow they all know. All of the grizzly bears, hundreds of them, in the Yellowstone National Park go to bed

on exactly the same day. By instinct they know which snow will be the final freeze of the winter even when man is not sure.

During their winter sleep many of the female bears give birth to one to four cubs. The mother watches her cubs carefully for as long as two years. During this time she teaches her cubs to hunt and take care of themselves.

Bears will attack very quickly if they feel that anyone is going to hurt their cubs. Bears are extremely strong and when angered will win a battle against practically anything.

Pity the poor person who might accidentally walk into the middle of a mother bear and her cubs. Her temper is so short, her arm so strong and her claws so sharp and fast that the unarmed visitor would have small chance.

But what is even more dangerous than a mother bear? A fool who is not careful what he says and does. He may hit someone in the eye while throwing stones. He may turn people against another person by telling lies. He might burn down a house because he plays with fire. Stay away from people who don't use good common sense. Sooner or later someone will get hurt by that fool.

1. How do bears know when to go to sleep?
2. Do bears like to fight?
3. When are people like mother bears?

It is safer to meet a bear robbed of her cubs than a fool caught in his folly.
—Proverbs 17:12

eighteen

A Worthless Worm

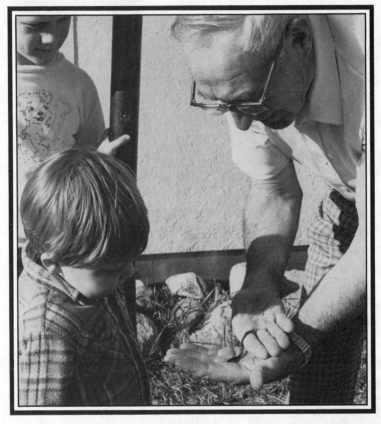

We can all be glad that people don't eat like earthworms. Every day a worm eats its own weight. A person would have to eat 60, 90 or even 200 pounds a day to keep up with a worm.

Worms don't have a fancy diet of pork chops and ice cream. They eat a daily dose of old leaves, and even a few helpings of dirt. When they dig holes they do it with their teeth by eating it as they go.

Rather than being a useless creepy little thing, the earthworm plays a very important part in nature. The ground needs worms to eat the vegetation and turn it into fertilizer so other things can grow. It leaves behind good portions of potassium, phosphorous and nitrogen to keep the earth rich.

Most worms are of the two- or three-inch variety, but some come much larger. In Australia there is a huge type which reaches eleven feet from tip to tip. Worms can be so useful to fertilize the ground and to help catch fish that some people have started "worm farms" for the purpose of raising them.

Without the worm our forests would become very hard and nearly empty places.

For years the worm has had a bad reputation. People refer to it as just an insignificant, useless creature, yet God made it as an important part of nature.

Job felt very small in the eyes of God. After all, why would the creator of an enormous universe be concerned about one man? That is like a fisherman taking care of a wounded earthworm.

But as small as one person is, God still cares. He cares so much that He sent His son to die for each person.

Worms are more important than they may appear and God uses them. Every person is important and God loves him.

1. How much does a worm eat daily?
2. How do worms help gardens?
3. Name one way you are important.

God is so glorious that even the moon and stars are less than nothing as compared to him. How much less is man, who is but a worm in his sight? — Job 25:5,6

nineteen

Where Do Rocks Come From?

Have you ever wished you were strong enough to bend a rock with your bare hands? Well, most of us are strong enough. That is, if we can get a rare rock called itacolumite. Found in North Carolina, it can actually be squeezed into different shapes.

However, most rocks are of a different substance. If we would hit a rock with our bare fist, our hand would almost always be the loser.

Most of us probably think of rocks as being old, and this is usually the case. However, they are also being formed today and sometimes before our eyes. For instance, a volcano throws out great gusts of hot

lava which cools and becomes rock. If someone could watch it long enough, he could see some fallen trees slowly turn into rock, which is called petrified wood. Other rocks are continuously being made, but they are not as easy to observe.

Most of the earth's surface or crust is made up of rocks. Possibly even 98% of the crust is rock. Even the ocean bottom is rock which has been covered over by vegetation, bones and other substances. Dry land is made up the same way.

The study of rocks is done by individuals, and there are many clubs all over the world which collect rocks. Those who study them professionally are called geologists. There are a lot of things yet unknown about this part of nature, but further studies may prove very helpful in supplying man's needs for tomorrow.

Rocks appear to be the most stable, unchangeable, dependable things on earth. Consequently, God is often compared with a rock. However, the truth is that God is far more dependable than rocks. Rocks melt, they shift and break; rocks are eaten away by the wind; rocks are broken into pieces by man. They are used to make iron and copper products and worn around the finger as diamonds.

Rocks were the strongest things David could compare God to, and yet God is far greater. God can be a constant companion, friend and help because nothing causes Him to shift or break down or move.

1. Where are rocks soft enough to bend?
2. How much of the earth's crust is rock?
3. How is God like a rock?

David sang this song to the Lord after he had rescued him from Saul and from all his other enemies: Jehovah is my rock, my fortress and my Savior.—2 Samuel 22:1, 2

twenty

Why Camels Have Humps!

After making a six-week visit to Arabia, a teacher said he found there is only one way to travel by camel. That is walking on the ground beside the animal.

Though the camel hump makes riding difficult for the newcomer, the hump really is very important to the camel. The camel is able to store fat in its hump when it eats and drinks well. When food is not available it lives off the resources accumulated on its back. The food and water have changed into molecules, and the camel can easily draw these into its system by adding oxygen.

If the camel has gone too long without supplies, the hump will begin to shrink in size as the animal lives off its contents. When the camel drinks and eats again, the hump will swell back to its original size.

This exceptional ability and adaptability to the hot weather make it an excellent animal for desert work and transportation. A camel can go a week to 10 days without food or water, but when it does drink it needs plenty. It can drink 25 gallons in just a matter of minutes.

The Bactrian Camel has two humps which make riding considerably easier. There are approximately one million camels in the world, and some scientists believe they once lived in North America.

The camel is six to seven feet tall and has thick, short fur. Their long legs allow them to carry large loads over great, hot distances. As a camel walks it causes a continuous shifting of its body. Therefore the

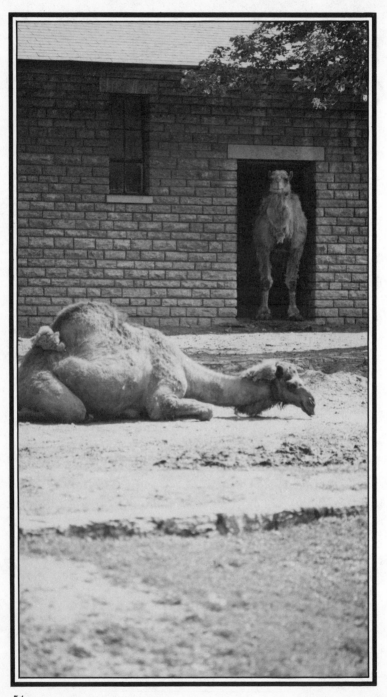

rider may feel a steady swaying, and the traveler can become "seasick" while going across the desert.

Not a picky eater, the camel will eat practically any plant in the desert. It can even bite off a thorny cactus and chew it without hurting its mouth.

We can't deny the fact that Jesus had a very good sense of humor. When He talked about a man swallowing a camel, seven feet tall, 1,000 pounds, hump and all, it is difficult to imagine a crazier sight. But then, Christ was telling the Pharisees that they were doing something just as ridiculous.

The Pharisees tried to keep a lot of little religious laws: don't touch this, don't go there, don't be seen with that person. They were careful about these things, like straining tiny gnats out of the soup. But, at the same time they refused to feed the hungry, clothe the poor, and be friends to the lonely. They were making such big mistakes that they looked as funny as if they were swallowing camels.

1. What are humps made of?
2. How much water can a camel drink?
3. Name one thing that is important for Christians to do. Explain.

Blind guides! You strain out a gnat and swallow a camel.—Matthew 23:24

twenty-one

Why Smoke Chokes

Have you ever sat in a small room next to someone puffing on a cigar and had the smoke drift into your face? Have you wondered why it makes you cough or why you can see smoke and not other forms of air?

When a cigar, a pile of trash or gasoline burns, heat rises as all hot air goes up. However, smoke is different from regular hot air and can be seen easily because it contains a substance called carbon. The carbon particles are very tiny, and as they float through the air they look for a place to land. They may come to rest on our clothes, our homes, our plants, our pets, or our skin. When they do land, these small specks start to discolor and sometimes even eat away at the material they settle on. They can eat away at clothing or even metal bridges over a period of time.

If smoke becomes very heavy and visible, it is called soot. When smoke mixes with fog it is called smog, which can be dangerous to health.

But there are several good uses for smoke. The Indians used it to send messages long before there was a telegraph or telephone. Smoke is also a good warning system to let us know there is a fire. It is used to cure meats or to keep certain plants warm on terribly cold nights.

However, presently there is far more damage than good being done by smoke. Over one billion dollars per year is wasted because of the bad effects of smoke from cars, planes, trains, factories and homes. Safer ways must be found to burn things in our society.

Not only do throats not like smoke, but eyes are not fond of it either. That is why our eyes sting, water and blink when we are around it. Smoke makes us uncomfortable as well as unhealthy.

Trying to work next to a lazy person has the same effect. We want to get the project done, but our partner just wants to talk, get a drink of water or pull tricks on people. When he grows up he probably will have trouble keeping a job since most employers don't like to be irritated by such people.

1. What is smog?
2. What makes it easy to see smoke?
3. Describe yourself as a worker.

A lazy fellow is a pain to his employers — like smoke in their eyes or vinegar that sets the teeth on edge. —Proverbs 10:26

twenty-two

The Mysterious Shark

The seas are filled with large, awesome and sometimes strange looking creatures, but of all of them only the shark is really dangerous to man. And yet, the shark may not be as fearsome as some stories make him appear.

While no one can be sure how many sharks there are, science has cataloged 250 species. Of these about 12% or 15% would attack a human being. Some sharks only grow to one foot in length and others are almost as large as whales. The huge species wouldn't hurt anyone. Normally the killer types range from 5 to 25 feet.

However, despite their general calm the famous authority on sharks, Jacques-Yves Cousteau, gives these two warnings: (1) The more we know about them, the less we know about them. (2) No one can ever tell what a shark might do.

Even the largest of sharks has a small brain for its enormous body. Baby sharks are born in numbers of 6 to 60 at one time. At birth they are up to 18 inches long and ready to take care of themselves.

Sharks love to eat and are not too picky about their meals. Scientists have found an odd assortment of things in sharks' stomachs: birds, turtles, coal, half a ham, a nylon raincoat, an automobile license plate, and more.

The shark appears to be a nervous creature. Actually it is constructed so it cannot stand still. Because of its tail and fins and lack of a swim bladder, the shark must keep moving or else it would sink like a rock.

Man is becoming more daring in his investigation of the shark. Men in iron cages are descending into the sea to get a closer look, and some men in scuba suits are going down with special protective weapons.

1. How many sharks are dangerous to people?
2. Name some things found in sharks' stomachs.
3. Can you think of animals that people mistreat?

So God created great sea creatures, and every sort of fish and every kind of bird. And God looked at them with pleasure, and blessed them all. "Multiply and stock the oceans," he told them, and to the birds he said, "Let your numbers increase. Fill the earth."—Genesis 1:21, 22

twenty-three

Bambi and Reindeer

There really is a reindeer, and it lives in the North of Europe, Asia and near the Arctic. They don't fly, but they are very important to local residents for food, clothing and utensils carved from their bones.

The deer is the name for a large family of animals which include elk, moose, caribou and such seldom known members as the little pudu. There are some 60 types all together. While some members are large and have strong antlers for fighting, most deer avoid all forms of combat. Their best defense is usually an excellent sense of smell and very fast legs. They are able to run at 40 miles per hour and leap 20 feet across a brook.

A deer's bite is different from many animals. Most types of deer have only bottom teeth in the front. The upper half is a thick, leathery pad. A complete set of teeth, however, are in the back of its mouth and are excellent for chewing.

While a deer does not have a regular home, it is more likely to have a territory. Within that area or forest it will roam, search for food, hide and mate.

For the young scientist looking for an animal to study, he might travel to South America and find the pudu or rabbit deer. It lives 10,000 feet up in the Andes Mountains, which explains why not many people have seen it. This deer is only one foot high and weighs 20 pounds soaking wet. It is complete with small antlers and hair. The pudu would be worth studying further.

The deer belongs to the group of animals which

chew their cud. When the deer eats its grass or leaves or moss, it doesn't chew it very well. Rather, it swallows its food into one of the four sections of its stomach. Later the deer brings the food up in a ball form and chews it as a meal. After this second chewing the food is swallowed again and this time it goes into another section of its stomach and is processed in its body.

It is easy to picture the "Bambi" looking deer standing by a quiet brook. It appears harmless and gentle. Very thirstily it drinks on a hot day. It is eager and glad to get its refreshment.

The psalm writer thinks about God and he remembers the deer standing by the brook. Then the writer says that just as much as the deer need water, that is how much we need God. That type of person has his ears open, his eyes ready, and his heart set. He wants to hear about God, to hear from God, and to live with Him daily.

1. Where does the one-foot-tall deer live?
2. What does it mean to chew its cud?
3. When you want to know more about God, where do you look?

As the deer pants for water, so I long for you, O God. I thirst for God, the living God. Where can I find him to come and stand before Him?—Psalm 42:1, 2

twenty-four

Egg White

The egg which most of us see on our breakfast plate is the contribution of a bird which worked all night just for us. Because of it we receive important amounts of protein, vitamins A, B and D and even are able to make some paint, ink, soap and varnish.

The chicken began working on this egg with just a tiny cell inside its body. The hen has enough of these cells to last its lifetime. This cell develops into the yellow yolk made up of six rings. A white liquid forms around the yolk and then tiny layers of shell surround the contents.

Some wild birds need a male bird to simply be present before it can form the egg. However, the farmer's chicken doesn't need a rooster. One hen laid 1515 eggs and never even saw a rooster.

If the egg is to hatch into a baby chick, two things

are necessary. First the male or rooster had to germinate the egg before it was laid. Second, the temperature of the egg must be raised to 99.5 degrees F in its center and the proper heat maintained for 21 days.

Job mentioned an interesting part of the egg: the uncooked white. This liquid part of the egg is not particularly good for man. It contains avidin which can slow a person's growth. If the egg goes on to become a chick, the unborn baby (embryo) feeds off this liquid.

From these verses in Job it is easy to see that he had become depressed. Life seemed useless, dull, even tasteless to him. If we can imagine eating uncooked egg white, it is easy to appreciate how sickening it had become. But then, sometimes life gets that way for all of us. Things are going badly for us, we are bored, we don't feel like doing anything. We have the blahs!

But even then God hasn't abandoned us. Tomorrow the sun will shine merely because there is a God who cares. Maybe we need to ask Him to help us get through the blahs.

1. How many rings are in a yoke?
2. What vitamins are in eggs?
3. How can God make your tomorrow more interesting?

For the Lord has struck me down with arrows deep within my heart. All God's terrors are arrayed against me. When wild donkeys bray, it is because their grass is gone; oxen do not low when they have food; a man complains when there is no salt in his food. And how tasteless is the uncooked white of an egg—my appetite is is gone when I look at it; I gag at the thought of eating it. — Job 6:4-7

twenty-five

The Underwater Forest

Probably Jonah didn't see much humor in this, but the description is a pretty funny sight. There goes the poor prophet on his way down with only a crown of seaweed decking his head.

This picture leads the reader to the natural question: What possible good is seaweed? Most of us see it only as a nuisance. It gets caught on our fishing lines and wraps around our legs when we go swimming. Yet, God built seaweed as possibly the most important feature of the sea.

Basically underwater vegetation serves the same purpose as it does on land. Seaweed produces oxygen for the fish and other marine life to breathe. Without this supply it would be impossible for anything to live there, and that is why many scientists feel that God had to create seaweed before the other ocean creatures.

Seaweed also serves as food for millions of different underwater inhabitants. These natural "farms" make the "supermarkets" which are necessary for water animals.

Scientists are now discovering many uses for seaweed to help man. Seaweed is plentiful in vitamins A, B, C, and some people regularly eat a bowl of seaweed soup. The day may not be far away when we will eat it.

Farmers have discovered that seaweed makes an excellent fertilizer. It contains nitrates, phosphates, potash, and manganese which crops need very much.

One dairyman in the United States fed his cows a supplement of dried seaweed and he won the world's record for milk production.

As George Washington Carver discovered so many uses for peanuts and sweet potatoes, the whole world of seaweed is being used in light bulbs, soap powder, hair lotions, shaving creams, aspirin and clothing. Moss is now being used to make ice cream and chocolate milk. Can you imagine someday ordering a moss milk shake?

1. How does seaweed help fish?
2. How can people use seaweed?
3. Can you name some other little things God created which are important?

I sank beneath the waves, and death was very near. The waters closed above me; the seaweed wrapped itself around my head.—Jonah 2:5

twenty-six

Snakes for Pets?

Someone has said that it is difficult to find anyone who really likes the slithery snake. It is too bad that the snake has been considered a villain, because most of them are really man's friends.

Many people have cats around their farms to keep the mouse population down. However, they might be better off to keep a pet snake. Snakes have huge appetites and eat as many as 150 rats and mice each month.

Snakes differ greatly in size. Some are smaller than the palm of a hand, while the world's largest snake, the Reticulate Python, may grow to 30 feet. If an owner takes good care of a viper (snake) it may live for 20 to 30 years. If someone did have a snake for a pet, it would be easy to care for, as they can go from one month to one year without eating if necessary.

The snake has earned part of its reputation as a monster because some are poisonous. Certainly, people should keep a safe distance from any snake they cannot identify. While nine out of ten snakes are harmless, there are some that are extremely dangerous.

The poisonous viper has fangs that operate like needles when it bites someone. These "needles" send a deadly chemical into the body and cause a harsh sting. Anyone who is bitten by a snake should seek a doctor or other help immediately.

Snakes are not the only creatures which send poison out of their mouths. People can be just as dangerous by the careless and cruel things they say. They tell lies, spread rumors and start gossip which does more harm than all the world's snakes. God is more concerned about the damage we do with our poisonous tongues than He is with all the snakes in the world.

1. Why are snakes important?
2. How do fangs work?
3. How do we spread poison?

Their talk is foul and filthy like the stench from an open grave. Their tongues are loaded with lies. Everything they say has in it the sting and poison of deadly snakes. — Romans 3:13

twenty-seven

Do We Have to Go to Bed?

Most children and quite a few adults resist going to bed and think they would enjoy staying up as late as possible. Nevertheless, people need a certain amount of sleep or else their bodies will protest by becoming weak and sick.

Usually when people sleep they lie down and close their eyes. Of course, if we were fish we could sleep with our eyes open. If we were horses we could take a nap standing up, and if we were bats we could even sleep upside down. Since we are human beings a good night of around eight hours of bedrest seems to work pretty well. Eight hours is by no means the perfect number. Some people can get by on less and others need ten or more. It is much like shoe sizes, and we are all a little different.

When we go to bed we very seldom go to sleep all at once. Maybe our muscles will begin to relax, our heart start to slow down, our sight and smell start to decrease. Soon our body, mind and heart reach a stage where they are calm enough to allow for a state of sleep.

Many of us used to think that the use of covers at night was just a habit, but evidently not. While we are sleeping our body is less active, and consequently our body temperature drops during the night making some cover usually preferable.

There are several reasons why we need regular sleep. For one thing, the body wears out a certain number of cells each day. It then needs the rest to

rebuild those cells. Sleep is also necessary to help the body grow. Therefore adults usually need less sleep than children.

While we may think we change positions once or twice during the night, in all probability we shift as many as a dozen times before morning. When someone does not sleep for long periods of time, his body rebels and often the person will become cranky and have difficulty thinking.

Some people seem to resist sleep because their minds remain too active for rest. They may be anxious or are worrying about tomorrow and they stay tense both in mind and body. Sometimes children are afraid of the night or are still jumpy over a television show they watched that evening.

The author of the fourth psalm has come to realize that even though he is alone there is nothing to fear. God watches over him and he can put his head down in peace.

1. Why are covers important?
2. How much sleep do you need?
3. Where is God while you are sleeping?

I will lie down in peace and sleep, for though I am alone, O Lord, you will keep me safe.—Psalm 4:8

twenty-eight

The Soaring Eagle

The title "King of the Birds" goes to the majestic and powerful eagle. He has long been a symbol of freedom and bravery. The ancient Romans used the eagle figure on their flags and weapons.

There are 48 different types of eagles, and they live in practically every part of the world. They make their nests very high and some of their homes are enormous, ranging to nine feet in diameter and weighing as much as two tons (over 4,000 pounds).

As with other birds they have an amazing construction, much like a small airplaine but in some ways even better. For instance, the African Eagle can swoop down on his prey at 100 miles per hour and come to a complete stop within 20 feet from the point he applied his brakes. Birds have a special landing mechanism in their legs. There are three single rigid bones with joints that move in opposite directions. Consequently they may have the best shock absorber system in all of nature.

Eagles are amazingly strong. Usually they weigh from eight to thirteen pounds and they can pick up food equal to their own weight. They then carry it high into the trees or mountains. The Harpy Eagle of South America hunts monkeys and sloths.

They are such good and graceful fliers that the Golden Eagle can cover a territory up to 60 miles searching for food. Some sheep farmers are afraid that Golden Eagles steal young lambs.

Some eagles, especially the Bald Eagle, are in dan-

ger of becoming extinct. While he faces few dangers from the animal world, his greatest enemy may be man. While in most states it is illegal to kill eagles, they are still dying off from the use of chemicals and other causes.

Anyone who has watched the effortless beauty of a soaring eagle can appreciate what the prophet Isaiah is saying. There are things which people believe they cannot possibly do. They cannot stop teasing or they cannot stop stealing or they cannot learn to treat people kindly and be helpful. But the prophet says that God can give a special strength so that we can do things we never dreamed we could. Watch the eagle soar; he is free and able just as God would like to make us.

1. How fast is the African Eagle?
2. How strong are eagles?
3. If God gave you the ability, what would you like to do?

But they that wait upon the Lord shall renew their strength. They shall mount up with wings like eagles; they shall run and not be weary; they shall walk and not faint. Isaiah 40:31

twenty-nine

The Moon Fools Us

The moon has always been of interest to mankind. It is our closest neighbor in space. Some people have been afraid it might collide with the earth, and others have thought it was God. Putting people on the moon used to be considered just a wild joke that few took seriously.

When we say the moon is close we don't mean it is only a couple of miles away. In fact, as it orbits around the earth, it never gets nearer than 225,742 miles away. The moon is smaller than the earth, about one-fourth the size.

The moon seems to most of us to be moving very slowly, just sitting in the sky like a lazy lion taking a nap. It only looks lackadaisical because it is so far away. Actually it is racing around the earth at 2,300 miles per hour. At that rate it takes 27 1/3 days to get around the earth.

Another way the moon fools people is that it appears to be shining at night. The truth is that the moon is dark and has no light of its own. The moon is really acting as a mirror and shows us the light from the sun.

The word "month" comes from moon because that is approximately how long it takes for it to complete its journey around the earth. As the moon travels around the earth it also rotates. Consequently, we see only one side of the moon and the "backside" always remains hidden from us.

Living on the moon would be difficult. There is no water, food or air on the moon, and a space capsule would be necessary to keep man alive.

There are many theories of how old the moon is and how it was made. Did it break off another planet? Was it a fireball that cooled? Or did God merely say "I want a moon" and zap a moon out of nothing? Whatever the mechanics, we believe that God made the moon and hung it over the earth. Sometimes when we wonder whether or not God really cares about us, we might just look up at the sky on a clear night. According to the psalm writer, as long as the moon remains, God will continue to love us. That kind of love is pretty easy to accept.

1. How close does the moon get to the earth?
2. How does the moon shine?
3. What does the moon remind us about God?

Praise him who made the heavenly lights, for his lovingkindness continues forever: the sun to rule the day, for his lovingkindness continues forever; and the moon and stars at night, for his lovingkindness continues forever.—Psalm 136:7-9

thirty

The Sly Fox

Any discussion of intelligent animals must eventually lead to the crafty, sly fox. It is doubtful that there is a smarter or more daring creature in all of nature.

While most animals fear man and dislike being hunted, there are some foxes which love to be chased. They have so much confidence in their ability to get away that they may show themselves to the hunter and dare him to try and catch him.

So far the fox is getting away with his little game. In the United States there is now one fox per every 50 acres, while 100 years ago there was one for every 173 acres. If a fox finds a trap that has been set, he may choose to play with it. Not only will he get away, he may also pull the chain to set off the trap just to laugh at the hunter.

A fox will take very good care of its baby pups. It doesn't merely push them out of the den at a certain age. Rather, the fox will give them thorough training in how to hunt for food. They even spend time practicing how to sneak up on something and how to make the final plunge.

Basically a night creature, the fox is greatly disliked especially by the farmer. While it enjoys eating some insects and fruit, it also has a tremendous love for chickens and ducks as well as quail and rabbits and other small game. It doesn't take very long to become unpopular around a farm.

At first a fox's home seems like a simple hole in the ground, but again he is clever. The fox builds two or three entrances into his underground apartment house. Then he will add several false tunnels which lead nowhere just to keep his enemies guessing.

There were plenty of smart little foxes running around during the time of Jesus, so He knew everyone was familiar with them. There were so many of them that they seemed like insignificant pests.

Jesus reminded His disciples that foxes do not lack places to live, and yet His followers may have to sacrifice everything. Some may have to leave their friends and homes because God wants to use them someplace else.

1. What does a fox eat?
2. Is the fox becoming extinct?
3. What do we give to help others?

But Jesus said, "Foxes have dens and birds have nests, but I, the Messiah, have no home of my own—no place to lay my head."—Matthew 8:20

thirty-one

The Big Eater

Most people don't want a bad reputation, and yet some can really get one. Like the person who lies, or a boy who steals and can't be trusted. Well, it would be hard to find anyone with a worse reputation than the big-eating moth.

There is no one insect which is a moth. Actually there are possibly 15,000 different types of moths. The mother moth lays its eggs on plants or on other material that her children (larva) can eat when they leave their eggs. When one hatches it starts earning its reputation immediately by eating the eggshell it just left. Then it begins to eat the material or plant where it is living.

Right after birth the moth does most of its damage and that destruction is considerable. Usually we think of a moth eating clothing, but this is only a small part of its task. If it is placed in certain areas it will eat trees, crops and other vegetation.

Moths that eat clothing are very destructive and difficult to get rid of. Destroying an adult moth in flight may help a little, but the real problems are the eggs which have already been laid. When they hatch, the clothes, carpets or upholstered chairs are already in trouble.

Not all moths are harmful, and some in fact are very valuable. For instance, the giant silkworm moth helps produce silk which is the strongest of natural fibers. A thread of silk is as strong as steel the same size. However, even this moth has a monumental appetite. The silk farmer feeds them mulberry leaves and they eat almost nonstop day and night.

While moths can be helpful, it is easy to understand why they bear watching and are often destroyed by people.

The moth which flies around a street light or porch bulb at night is a good reminder of how quickly things are destroyed in life. One moth laying eggs could ruin an expensive suit or put holes in a beautiful rug.

God wants to warn us that we shouldn't put all of our efforts into things that may be here today and gone tomorrow. The only things which will never rust, be torn down, be burned up or be ruined by bugs are the things we do as service to God: helping people, comforting the sick, feeding the poor, sharing Jesus Christ. These things will last forever.

1. Which mothers are helpful?
2. What is a larva?
3. What things last forever?

Your wealth is even now rotting away, and your fine clothes are becoming mere moth-eaten rags.—James 5:2

thirty-two

Nature's Hero

The real story behind every seed is a story of courage. Often seeds are tiny but they are tough and don't give up easily.

If you ever see a large brown ball on the ground, don't kick it until you check closely; it might be a seed. The seed for a coconut tree weighs 22 pounds and could give someone a very sore toe.

Seeds come in a large variety of shapes and sizes. Some look like hairy little bugs or beetles. Others, like onion seeds, resemble an upside-down light bulb. Not all plants need seeds, but most of them begin this way.

The average seed has a tough battle ahead if it is going to become a plant. For one thing, there are a lot of birds flying around looking for helpless seeds for breakfast. There are winds and breezes which pick them up and carry them to some unknown part of the land. Then a seed must find its way into the dark ground before it can start to grow.

Once in the ground a seed has to receive just the right amount of rain. Too little rain will cause it to dry up and too much may cause it to rot.

In spite of these tough conditions, seeds do not give up easily. They even take these dangers and use them to help growth. Sometimes they have to be very patient before they are able to send a small sprout out of the ground. Most seeds do best within their first year, but a cucumber seed can wait ten years before being planted and some wheat still grew after 30 years.

The seed is a story of nature which is willing to try even when the going is hard.

If a seed could think, it might look at all of the obstacles it has to face and just give up. Sometimes people do just that. They are sure they can't learn mathematics or get a part in the play or make the track team, so they don't even try. The Bible says keep on trying, plant those seeds, and you will be surprised how many good things will happen.

1. How big are coconut tree seeds?
2. How do seeds get from place to place?
3. Do you like to try new things? Like what?

Keep on sowing your seed, for you never know which will grow—perhaps it all will.—Ecclesiastes 11:6

thirty-three

The Family Hunter

The wolf is a handsome animal with gorgeous fur, but unfortunately it has earned a terrible reputation. Cartoons, books and fairy tales depict it as the big bad wolf who steals and destroys.

Some of this reputation is well earned. Wolves will attack sheep and other livestock as well as wild game. Farmers and ranchers try to kill them off, and in some areas rewards are offered for shooting or trapping a wolf. It does appear that wolves will kill more than they can eat and this only adds to his role as a villain.

The wolf is a close relative to the fox and dog, and consequently his appearance and some of his habits are smiliar. They dig dens in the ground to give birth to their pups, and like the fox they carefully train their offspring before they let them go out on their own. Their immediate family ties are very strong. They usually choose one mate and remain with it for life.

The packs of wolves which are so famous are very often merely a family of a mother and father and their four to six pups traveling together. On other occasions they may hunt alone or in pairs.

Weighing around 100 pounds, the wolf has excellent speed and endurance. It is capable of running for hours at 20 miles per hour. Consequently, it could cover 100 to 200 miles in a given day if necessary. Its dark and sinister image is partly due to the fact that it will often wait and attack at night.

Animal lovers insist that the wolf plays an important role in the balance of nature. However, those who

lose livestock to wolves are very eager to get rid of them. The result is that the wolf is very hard to find in many parts of the world. While they are found in the United States and Canada, they are restricted mostly to the northern and mountainous regions.

Few scenes are less likely to happen than to see a wolf and a sheep settle down together. The sheep's instinct will be to run, and the wolf's impulse will be to attack. Jesus realized that everyone knew this fact since wolves and sheep were part of the country of Palestine. Using this illustration Jesus warned that there are teachers in life who pretend to be our friends but underneath their disguise they are really wolves who only want to hurt us.

Maybe they tell us that stealing is all right. Maybe they tell us that lying is what everyone does. Maybe they even teach us that we are better than some races or nationalities of people. Maybe they teach us to hate people of another religion.

Jesus says, "Watch out." They talk smoothly and they sound sincere, but in the end they will only hurt us.

1. Who are the wolves' relatives?
2. Why do many farmers dislike wolves?
3. Why did Jesus warn us about wolves?

Beware of false teachers who come disguised as harmless sheep, but are wolves and will tear you apart.—Matthew 7:15

thirty-four

Pencils and Canoes

What do canoes, pencils, sauna baths and house roofs all have in common? Often the wood for these comes from an American cedar tree. It makes ideal pencils because it sharpens well, and works well for canoes because it is warp resistant. Grandmother might even have a good cedar chest to store blankets in because the cedar wards off moths.

The cedar trees in America are related to the cedars of Lebanon so often mentioned in the Bible. They have a fresh, sweet odor and a tough reddish wood. They look much like a pine tree and have similar pine cones which house seeds.

Because of its special toughness ancient kings such as Solomon used the wood for special buildings in Israel. Hiram, the king of Tyre, agreed to furnish the lumber in large amounts. Consequently, they were cut down in Lebanon, tied into huge rafts, and with men riding on them floated to Israel on the Mediterranean Sea.

We don't know how much wood was used in Israel, but we do know that as many as 80,000 men were engaged at different times in cutting the lumber and shaping it into buildings and carvings. David built his lovely palace from cedar and Solomon constructed the temple of Israel from the same type of wood. Solomon later spent thirteen years building his own house of the valuable cedar. His personal living quarters were paneled with a beautiful cedar wood.

The cedar tree grows well in America and is often an expensive wood. Because of its durability, beauty

and fine smell, it is a highly prized material. The actual cedars of Lebanon have not been taken care of very well and have been cut down very freely. Consequently, there are not many left of what once were vast forests of bluish-green trees.

To the Israelite the cedars of Lebanon represented strength, beauty and value. Therefore if they wanted to pay something a real compliment, instead of saying it was "as good as gold" they might say "as lovely as a cedar from Lebanon." A young lady might say her boyfriend was like the cedars of Lebanon, and everyone knew she loved him (Song of Solomon 5:15).

Likewise, when someone wanted to say that God would take good care of them, they might say, "God will make me like the cedars of Lebanon." This could mean that God would give them good health, lots of money, a happy family or a good many other things. It merely meant that God had been good to me.

1. How long did Solomon take to build his house?
2. Where did Israel get its beautiful cedars?
3. Name three good things God has given you.

But the godly shall flourish like palm trees, and grow tall as the Cedars of Lebanon. For they are transplanted into the Lord's own garden, and are under his personal care. — Psalm 92:12, 13

thirty-five

Pigs Are Really Clean Animals

The American Indian never saw a hog before ships started bringing them here from England and Spain almost 500 years ago. Today there are many millions of hogs raised all over the United States.

Hogs have a bad reputation for being very dirty animals and loving to roll in the mud. While they do enjoy a nice mud bath, they are actually cleaner than most other animals and are very intelligent.

They might be willing to give up the mud bath except that they have a physical problem. The thick skin has no sweat glands, so it runs the risk of overheating. Since a hog has no built-in air-conditioning, it has to find some relief in the hot summer and looks for water wherever it can be found.

Hogs are not big fighters since they don't have fast legs or sharp claws. They can't see very well and even their large teeth (tusks) are often clipped off by farmers. Consequently, about the only defense the slow swine has is to run away.

In the days when hogs roamed wild (and some still do), they found their food by digging for vegetable roots. Since they don't have claws to dig with, they use their noses to break open the ground. Its nose is called a snout, is large and leathery and naturally used for breathing.

Because of this habit of digging for roots, a pig was a particularly unpleasant animal to keep. Following its taste, the pig would make large holes all over the farmer's yard in search of treats. To discourage the animal from "rooting," the owner would place

a metal ring in the hog's nose. Consequently, when it tried to dig, its nose would hurt and the pig would back off.

Obviously, the farmer wouldn't take his finest diamond ring and put it into a pig's nose. The ring would soon be dirty and ugly. Few people could appreciate the beauty of the jewel, and everyone would agree it was a terrible waste of something very valuable.

A young lady who is brash, who insults people and talks without thinking is the same type of waste. She has every reason to be beautiful, but her actions only make her look unpleasant. The really lovely people in life are the ones who are kind and considerate. The ones who enjoy being cruel and nasty lose their beauty under the mud.

The same principle applies to young men.

1. Why do hogs need mud baths?
2. How does a pig use its nose?
3. How does a rude, harsh person make you feel?

A beautiful woman lacking discretion and modesty is like a fine gold ring in a pig's snout. — Proverbs 11:22

thirty-six

Waterless Clouds

Clouds are one of the most familiar sights to people in practically every part of the world. They serve as an almost daily parade marching across the skies. Sometimes clouds mean it is going to rain; other times, snow; and other times they merely move on without leaving a drop.

Of course, clouds don't really come from the sky. They actually come from the earth and then form overhead. When the sun beams down on a lake or river, the temperature of the water rises and very small particles or vapor escape into the air. As an experiment, put a bucket of water in the backyard in warm weather. Each day you will notice there is less water in the bucket.

This water in vapor form goes up into the air, and when enough vapor gathers together and cools it forms a cloud. Clouds usually stay from about three miles to ten miles above the earth.

When wind catches the clouds, it sends them across the sky. However, on some days they do not seem to be moving at all.

A cloud will send rain when it has become heavy with particles of water. These begin as very tiny particles that collide with other particles and form raindrops by the time they reach the earth. If the temperature of a cloud drops to about 0 degrees F, crystals will fall. These crystals have a slight amount of water in them, and when they collide in the air they turn into snowflakes.

On a hot, dry day we sometimes see clouds moving over our heads. The grass, the garden and the farms all need rain, but somehow the clouds just pass over without sending a drop. Sometimes people disappoint us just like passing clouds. They talk about being good friends and they make a lot of promises, but when we need them they turn out to be empty. Jude says that some people talk a great deal about following Christ; but when the tough times come, they are like clouds which move too quickly past us without leaving a drop.

1. Where do clouds begin?
2. How high are clouds?
3. When did you last help a friend?

When these men join you at the love feasts at the church, they are evil smears among you, laughing and carrying on, gorging and stuffing themselves without a thought for others. They are like clouds blowing over dry land without giving rain, promising much, but producing nothing.—Jude 12a

thirty-seven

The King of Beasts

One of nature's sights of majestic beauty is the male lion with full mane crowning his head. It is easier to appreciate him if he is in a picture or safely behind some bars at the local zoo. In person he is one of the strongest and fastest animals in the jungle.

Lions may reach three and one-half feet high and nine and one-half feet long. One lion may weigh in at 500 pounds and be able to leap more than 20 feet through the air. Just to hear him roar sends fear through his fellow animals.

With little regard for size or speed, the lion may make practically any animal its prey. It will attack the speedy antelope or with equal agility bring down a full-grown elephant or hippopotamus. In fact, the lion would have had very few natural enemies except for man, and hunters have completely eliminated them from some areas of the earth.

One wouldn't think it needed much help, but the lion does not usually hunt alone. They travel in groups called prides, consisting of four or five and sometimes numbering into the twenties. An excellent hunter, it knows how to break the neck of its victim with the single blow of a paw.

After a hunt the other lions will back away from the stricken meal and allow the male lion to eat first. However, the female has probably done most of the work during the hunt.

Lions live long lives, often reaching 20 to 30 years

old. The male will grow his striking mane at around the age of five.

A lion is very strong and difficult to bring down, even with a rifle. It will usually take several shots to bring one down unless it is shot in the brain. In most cases it would take an expert shot to bring down an onrushing lion.

Despite his obvious abilities, this member of the cat family is a very lazy animal. He may sleep on his back like a human, and after a hunt may "sack out" for four days.

Lions are so powerful that they are not frightened off easily. When they capture a meal they take their

time and eat it patiently with little regard for any other creature that might come around.

When God decides to help His people He develops the same immoveable attitude. He has promised to take care of us and guard us. No one will cause Him to run away.

1. Who hunts lions?
2. How big are lions?
3. Does God ever leave us? Explain.

But the Lord has told me this: When a lion, even a young one, kills a sheep, he pays no attention to the shepherd's shouts and noise. He goes right on and eats. In such manner the Lord will come and fight upon Mount Zion. He will not be frightened away! He, the Lord of Hosts, will hover over Jerusalem as birds hover round their nests, and he will defend the city and deliver it. —Isaiah 31:4, 5

thirty-eight

Apple of His Eye

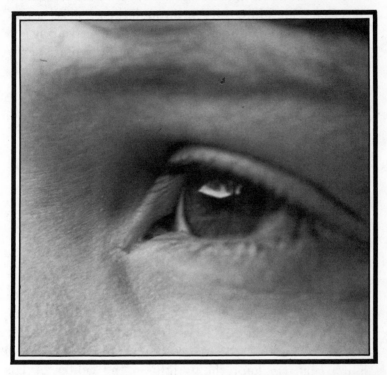

There are a lot of strange sayings in the English language. For instance, where did "sicker than a dog" come from? Who started calling people "chicken"? We call these odd sayings idioms.

The Bible uses a strange phrase, "apple of his eye." Does this have to do with apples or eyes, or neither one?

Despite the small size of the eye, it is a very complicated and carefully made part of the body. It consists of nerves, muscles, lens and a shutter called an iris.

The eye has five major parts. The *cornea* is the transparent part which covers the entire eye. The colored circle part of the eye is the *iris*. The dark center of the eye is called the *pupil*. Behind the pupil is a *lens* which helps us to focus when we look at something close or far away. On the back of the eye is a *retina* which acts in the same way as a movie screen.

What comes into the eye through the pupil is flashed on the screen or the retina. Anything appearing on that screen is sent immediately through the optic nerve back to our brain and our brain reacts to the picture. The picture may make us happy, sad, or not stir up much reaction at all.

The center of the eye is the pupil. In order for us to see something, the picture has to enter that pupil. Consequently, the pupil is extremely important, and the English referred to it as the apple of their eye.

The human eye works on the same principle as the camera. However, even the best made and most expensive camera does not work as well as our eye.

God told the people of Israel that He loved them very much and they were very special to Him. Then when the English wanted to translate the Hebrew language into the English, they looked for their best phrase or idiom to describe God's love, and so they wrote "apple of his eye." It meant that God loved them so much that He kept them right in the center of His pupil. He won't take His eye off them.

Only God could give all of us this kind of individual attention and love. Nevertheless, He does it for all of us.

1. Name three of the five major parts of the eye.
2. What is the center of the eye?
3. How does God show you His love?

God protected them in the howling wilderness as though they were the apple of his eye.—Deuteronomy 32:10

thirty-nine

Yak Butter

In the far-off country of Tibet there lives a member of the ox family called a yak. A sturdy hump-back work animal, a yak plays a very important role in life.

Though it isn't a fast animal, it is so tame it can be easily saddled and used for transportation. A Tibetan would hate to lose his yak. It supplies meat for him, warm clothing, and a good tent.

The yak also furnishes money for its owner. The animal's milk is churned into yak butter which is used for cash. Consequently, a Tibetan will take a few pounds of yak butter to pay his rent or haul a gallon of yak butter to settle up his taxes. They also use the butter to give religious offerings. When they want to make decorations, they might carve a nice statue out of this same ox product.

When Tibetans aren't passing yak butter around, they are eating and drinking it by the pound. The average person may drink as much as 50 cups of buttered tea per day. Tourists find it difficult to swallow at all, but the local people seemingly can't get enough.

Because the Tibetan often lives in the freezing mountains, the butter gives him fat which he needs to keep him warm. The owner is so dependent on the yak that he even uses its body waste—dung—as fuel to heat his home.

Members of the ox family are noted for their strength and many uses, but they are not famous for their intelligence. Nevertheless, this beast of burden soon learns to identify its master. The ox knows who feeds, waters and protects it, and the ox establishes a closeness to his master.

Man often doesn't show the common sense of the brute yak. The ox has learned to be faithful to the person who takes care of it. Man frequently forgets the God who keeps him. He may refuse to worship or serve his God and in fact may ignore Him altogether.

1. How are yaks used?
2. How do Tibetans pay their taxes?
3. Name two ways we could serve God.

The children I raised and cared for so long and tenderly have turned against me. Even the animals—the donkey and the ox—know their owner and appreciate his care for them, but not my people Israel. No matter what I do for them, they still don't care.—Isaiah 1:2, 3

forty

The Center of the Earth

We talk about trips to outer space and walking on the ocean floor, but there is yet another fascinating place to explore. What would people find if they could travel into the center of the earth?

The earth on which we live is an amazing place. We know a lot about its structure, and there is also a lot that is still a mystery. If we could cut the earth in half down the middle like a golf ball, we would find it is made of four sections.

First is the crust upon which we live. It ranges from 20-40 miles thick which really isn't much. Second comes a mantle which is 1,800 miles. It is thicker than the crust and made up of heavy rock. Third comes the outer core measuring 1,375 miles, which may be a softer material, possibly even liquid. Fourth is the inner core of 800 miles. This section may be solid.

Easy mathematics tell us the earth is approximately 3,615 miles from your house to the very center. That would make it about 7,230 miles across the inside.

Since we have never traveled deeply into the earth, some of these facts have been learned by using a seismograph. This instrument helps measure how thick, thin, solid or liquid something might be. Other things are just guesses because they are difficult to check.

It does appear that the earth gets hotter the closer one gets to the center. Miners report an increase in temperature as they go deeper. If the surface measurements are correct the earth is hotter by one degree each 60 feet deep. This is purely a guess, but if it

grew hotter at that rate the center of the earth would be 350,000 degrees hot. That would make the center of the earth 35 times as hot as the sun. Many scientists think this is impossible, and in the future much more study will be needed to look into the mystery of the earth.

While we don't have all the answers about *what* the earth is like, we can be very sure *why* there is an earth. God decided that He wanted to create a beautiful planet for people to live on. Far from being an accident of nature, God knew the earth was a good idea, and the Bible teaches us that Jesus Christ helped put it all together (John 1:1).

It's too bad that some people have made the earth an evil place by hate and violence. God would still like to have us make the earth the great and good place He planned for it to be.

1. What is the earth's crust?
2. What is a seismograph?
3. How could Christians help make this a better world?

The Lord's wisdom founded the earth; his understanding established all the universe and space. The deep fountains of the earth were broken up by his knowledge, and the skies poured down rain.—Proverbs 3:19, 20

forty-one

How Much Sand Is There?

Anyone who has ever walked along a beach, driven across a desert, played on a riverbed, or looked across the small hills of Nebraska must be convinced of one thing: there is a lot of sand in the world.

But where does all this sand come from, and what is it made from? Every grain of sand was once a part of a large mass of rock. As the wind or water beat against the rock small pieces were broken off and rolled away. As millions of these tiny pieces collect together, they form a sandy beach or a desert. Consequently, sand is being made all over the world all of the time.

Some sand is made under the seas, oceans or rivers, but probably not most of it. Many geologists believe that practically all of the smooth sand had to be blown smooth above the water and later find its way into the water. They think a grain of sand would have to travel a distance equal to 50 times around the world in order to become smooth under water.

If anything in the world is uncountable, sand must come close to it. There are deserts covering thousands of square miles which are piled high with just sand. There are old towns which have been completely covered by sand. There are sand dunes (giant hills) in Saudi Arabia, made of just sand, taller than the Washington Monument. Even some scientists scratch their heads in amazement that there could be so much sand in the world.

Naturally, sand is not very large. In order to be

called sand it has to measure less than one-twelfth of an inch, and none of us would have difficulty lifting a grain of sand. However, imagine a bushel basketful of sand. It would be just as heavy as a huge rock the size of a basket. There are a lot of us who couldn't lift a bushel of sand.

All of us have problems both large and small and we try our best to handle those difficulties. But the Bible says that the person who is a rebel has more problems than he can carry. A rebel is someone who finds fault with everything, doesn't get along with others, and is against anything others want to do. He is always upsetting his parents, his friends, and his teachers.

This person doesn't have a few little problems like the sand. He is collecting a bushel basket and will probably be unhappy because his difficulties are getting too heavy.

1. How is sand made?
2. How high do sand dunes become?
3. How can Christ help take problems away?

A rebel's frustrations are heavier than sand and rocks.—Proverbs 27:3

forty-two

The Living Desert

Man must always think twice before he moves out into the hot desert. People need water, and when they trespass onto a land of relentless heat they may be in more trouble than they can handle.

If the average healthy man is left on a hot desert under full heat, he probably will not be alive at the end of the day. If the temperature reaches 120 degrees, he will likely lose one quart of perspiration in the first hour along with valuable salt. He may lose up to 20 pounds the first day. If the temperature is less and he has some water, that same person might live as long as a week.

Some people have learned to adapt to such enormous heat by adjusting their clothes, but most fair-skinned people will find it very difficult. Even those who are accustomed to the heat can be fooled and perish. In 1805 a caravan of 2,000 men and 1,800 camels all died as they crossed a desert where all of the water holes had dried up.

Despite the barren appearance of the desert, there is really much more life than most of us can see. One strange phenomenon of the desert is that there are shrimp eggs under the dry clay. On some American deserts after a heavy rain millions of fresh water shrimp can be seen on the barren ground. Some of these eggs have been lying quietly for as long as 100 years and at the right time have hatched when enough rain has been available. This may be good evidence that a lake once covered these desert areas.

However, for anything to survive in the harsh, dry land it has to develop a tough disposition. The animals would eat all of the plants if the cactus had not grown thorns to discourage its enemies. The small kangaroo rat has learned to survive without water. It takes its moisture from tiny seeds and then doesn't lose liquid because it has no sweat glands and doesn't urinate. In all, some 5,000 different species have learned to live very well on the barren wasteland.

Despite the hardships of the desert, man is using irrigation to bring water and turning large areas into farm lands and forests. But then, God promised man that the apparently useless desert could come to life with vegetation and lakes, and mines and gardens. Nothing is useless in the hands of God.

Sometimes people feel like deserts. They don't think they can do anything right. They think everyone is better than they are. They don't believe they have any talent.

In God's nature not even the desert is useless. How much more important are people than a vast dry land. There are a lot of things each of us is good for. God gave us all valuable gifts and talents that we could really enjoy using.

1. What are desert shrimp eggs?
2. How does a kangaroo survive?
3. Name two abilities God has given you.

The parched ground will become a pool, with springs of water in the thirsty land. Where desert jackals lived, there will be reeds and rushes! — Isaiah 35:7

forty-three

Do Whales Worry?

If you don't like to cook be glad you don't have to prepare a meal for a whale. The sperm whale eats half a ton of food every day. When an animal is 65 feet long and over 100 tons, it takes a few large meals just to keep it going.

Whales may eat giant squids, seals, sharks and even a few people if they get in the way. The whale will also pack in an assortment of anything else it happens to suck in. Smaller whales that have few or no teeth eat from the billions of tiny sea creatures, fish, shrimp and jellyfish which are plentiful in the ocean.

The baleen whale is one which eats in a fairly lazy fashion. It simply coasts through the water with its mouth partially open and thousands of small creatures end up in the giant jaws. Then the whale may simply close its mouth, force the water out and then swallow its meal. The baleen then opens its mouth and starts filling up again.

Because the growing season differs even under the ocean, the whales often stay on the move. They head for northern waters in the summer and turn south with the coming of winter.

During the first seven months of a whale's life, it is nursed just like cows, kittens and many human beings. It lives off milk from its mother until it is able to search for and chew sea creatures and plants.

There are some whales, called killer-whales, which travel in groups and will attack larger ones. They are 20 feet long and find their food by attacking their own kind. Killer-whales seem to fear nothing including boats and ships. Preferring the colder regions, they like to eat seals, walruses, porpoises and squid. Most whales are very peaceful but all of sea nature seems to step back for the whale.

With these gigantic appetites one would think that searching for food would be a tremendous problem for the whale. The whale has no cans of food or boxes of cereal. It can't depend on the local grocery store stocking half a ton of shrimp for it every day.

Nevertheless, does the whale worry about food? By no means. God put nature in balance so there would be plenty of food for everything. As long as that balance stays in check and man doesn't destroy it, the whale and everything else seem to have plenty to eat.

God has supplied enough food for a giant whale, and He has supplied enough for man also. If man will use his common sense and be humble before God, there should be plenty for us too.

1. What do whales eat?
2. Why do whales move to other areas?
3. What times worry people? How can God help them?

And look! See the ships! And over there, the whale you made to lay in the sea. Every one of these depends on you to give them daily food. You supply it, and they gather it. You open wide your hand to feed them and they are satisfied with all your bountiful provisions.—Psalm 104:26-28

forty-four

Why Fires Burn

Fires are fascinating to watch. People of all ages can be seen by the hours standing around a campfire just to see the colored flame and listen to the crackle.

But fires don't just happen. There have to be certain conditions before a flame will whip into shape. First, we need a piece of material that will burn. Second, we need heat which usually comes in the form of other fire. Third, we have to have plenty of oxygen which is found readily in air.

When these three aspects come together under the right circumstances, fire or burning are the result. In order to put a fire out, one of these three elements has to be removed: cut the air off, extinguish the heat, etc. This also explains the reasons why a fire can be increased by fanning air into it. Air is approximately 1/5 oxygen, and the amount of air affects the amount of fire.

Fire has to be treated with great respect because of the tremendous damage it can do. However, fire is also capable of being very helpful. Thomas Edison discovered that if a small amount of heat was controlled under the right conditions, it would give off light inside a small bulb. Consequently, he used electricity to heat a carbon filament until it became hot enough to send out light. On the basis of this knowledge he invented the first light bulb, which helped change the living habits of people all over the world. To check this principle at work, merely hold your hand a few inches below a bulb after it has been lit for a while and feel the heat which in turn produces the light.

Another important part of our formula to create

fire is the necessity for fuel. Not everything will burn. Sand, brick, stone, steel and copper will not burn under normal conditions because oxygen cannot get into the substance in sufficient amounts to support a flame.

If someone is really angry at another person, he may say, "Tony really burns me." Well, our friend isn't on fire; he is just good and mad at Tony. Consequently, he may say some pretty ugly things about him and even tell other people to stay away from Tony.

This is a foolish way to treat other people, but it seems that most of us—children and adults—do it a lot. God is concerned about this type of behavior and how we treat other people. So He had someone write these words to help us: "Fire goes out for lack of fuel." He was saying that if we stop spreading rumors and telling stories about people, we can start to forgive and forget whatever has happened. By continuing to talk about them we only keep a very damaging fire going. We need to remove the fuel by refusing to run the person down any longer. Then the fire will go out.

1. List three conditions for fire.
2. Why don't bricks normally burn?
3. How can we stop "fires" among people?

Fire goes out for lack of fuel, and tensions disappear when gossip stops.
—Proverbs 26:20

forty-five

King of Strength and Speed

How would you like to own a horse? Most children would like to at some time in their lives. Horses are beautiful animals and can be trained to do both tricks and also many helpful jobs.

Most horses in the world are owned and cared for by someone, but a few wild horses still roam freely. In some parts of Africa and Asia herds of horses, and their close relatives such as Zebras, run loose. However, these are becoming more scarce. There are still some wild horses in the United States which graze free, but they are the descendants of tame horses which were brought here by early settlers.

Horses vary in size from approximately 2,400 pounds down to a small pony weighing in at around 300 pounds. Despite its size and tremendous strength, the horse is ideally proportioned for running. Its high but strong legs allow it to reach excellent speeds. In 1950 a horse named Noor ran 1 1/4 miles in less than 2 minutes. This is twice the speed of the fastest man.

With the horse's great size, strength and speed comes a basically gentle personality. Though some horses naturally have sour dispositions, they are not basically hostile animals. They don't attack other animals for food and live a vegetarian life eating grass, grain and hay.

The old saying "He eats like a horse" is well earned by the horse. It eats several times a day and its stomach can hold 4 1/2 gallons of food. The average man's stomach holds only one quart. A horse may drink up to 20 gallons of water per day.

Horses seemed highly qualified for man to use for work and travel if man was able to control them. Mastering a one-ton animal that could run a mile in two minutes would be no easy job. In order to accomplish this, man devised a piece of material that fits into a horse's mouth and has ropes or leather tied to each side. This material, now made of metal, is called a bit. A bit doesn't hurt the horse but merely pulls at the corners of its mouth. The horse will turn or stop depending on how the gentle pressure is applied to the bit.

This remarkable invention allows a 60-pound child to control a horse 40 times his size. It only makes sense that if we can control something that large, it would be an easy matter to make a little tongue obey us. Yet, that tiny half-pound tongue is harder to train than the wildest of beasts. It moves a lot, hurts a lot of people, and helps us to say a good many dumb things.

A wild, untamed horse is useless and probably will run away. A wild, untamed tongue is worse because it stays around and does a lot of damage.

1. How much does a horse eat?
2. What are bits?
3. Have people said mean things about you? How do we talk about others?

If anyone can control his tongue, it proves that he has perfect control over himself in every other way. We can make a large horse turn around and go wherever we want by means of a small bit in his mouth.—James 3:2, 3

forty-six

The Bone Factory

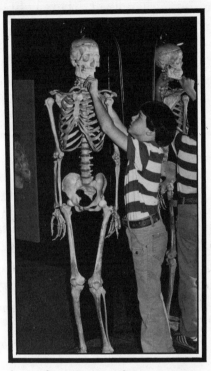

Long before a child is born from its mother a miraculous process has started to work. Inside the mother soft tissue has begun to change into firm and then hard pieces called bones. The change begins at the skull and then spreads to the rest of the body.

It would be easy to think that bones are just so many sticks connected together to hold up our skin, but actually bones do much more. In fact there is an entire factory fast at work inside the bone. This factory is called the marrow, and man couldn't live without it.

There is a red bone marrow which is busy making new blood all the time. An average adult loses two

115

ounces of blood each day, and that blood needs to be replaced. Consequently, this little factory has the job of producing approximately two million cells every second of every day. When people eat foods with plenty of iron, like liver, they help this factory do its terrific job.

Bones also play an important role in cleansing the blood. Along with other parts of the body, such as the kidneys and liver, the bones help sift out harmful elements which otherwise might travel through a person's system.

Healthy bones have a remarkable ability to repair themselves if they become broken. A special body "glue" will begin to form in the break and "cement" the bone back together. This healing material is called callus and consists of cartilage and new bone. In most breaks it is important to get a doctor to put the broken bone in its correct place before the glue starts to work.

Bones love good exercise. Especially when a child is growing the bones will become stronger because they have been put to good use.

The body is an easy system to take for granted. We live with it every day and we forget about the fascinating things it does. If it is properly cared for in most cases, it will continue to perform all of these wonders for many years.

1. What is our bone factory called?
2. Name the glue that cements our breaks.
3. Since our body is a gift from God, how should we care for it?

You gave me skin and flesh and knit together bones and sinews. You gave me life and were so kind and loving to me, and I was preserved by your care.—Job 10:11, 12

forty-seven

The Miracle of Migration

One of the most amazing feats in nature is the ability of animals and birds to move great distances and return months later to their exact home. Called "migration," these creatures move thousands of miles to places they have never seen before, finding their destination without the help of a compass, map and sometimes without landmarks.

Birds are an excellent example of this remarkable ability. For instance, an Arctic Tern at the tender age of six weeks can take off for a warmer home which is 11,000 miles away. When summer returns the fowl makes the huge journey back to find its nest again at the North Pole.

Scientists disagree on the reason why birds are able to do this. Are they trained? Do they follow the sun? Is the North Star the answer? So far none of these answers seems to cover all of the situations. The Romans used to believe the birds really turned into frogs. What they didn't realize was that the birds left at night while people were sleeping.

One gentleman tried to see how difficult he could make migration, so he took one Manx Shearwater from the coast of Wales. He isolated the bird and put a band on his leg. He then transported it to Boston, Massachusetts, and released it. Precisely 12 1/2 days later the shearwater arrived at its home 3,050 miles away. It had crossed the ocean without landmarks, all alone and still arrived safely home.

Many theories are still being discussed as to how this can happen, but so far there is no definite answer. Inside the bird's small brain there is a yet unexplained ability which may have to be called instinct. Whatever it is, we know God has equipped the bird and many other creatures with an internal "clock and compass" which leave men scratching their heads.

When God created nature He put certain abilities and instincts into it. Nature obeys these laws just as God mapped them out. Can we imagine a tree growing down into the ground instead of up? What would happen if someday it rained rocks? It doesn't happen because generally speaking nature obeys God, and even birds follow the instincts which were placed in them.

Now, if man only showed as much sense as nature. Instead of rebelling against God and hurting himself and others, man needs to follow Jesus Christ.

1. What did the Romans believe happened to birds?
2. How did a man try to fool a Manx Shearwater?
3. Why did God give us laws?

The stork knows the time of her migration, as does the turtledove, and the crane, and the swallow. They all return at God's appointed time each year; but not my people! They don't accept the laws of God.—Jeremiah 8:7

forty-eight

Mountain Climbers

Mountain goats can climb around on dangerous ledges where few people are able to go. They are such talented climbers that if necessary they can rear up on their two hind feet and turn completely around on the smallest area.

Not normally thought of as a fighting animal, goats are very capable at using their horns. When necessary a goat will fight a fierce grizzly bear and succeed in killing the beast.

At times goats live a lonely life. They live at high altitudes where the cold is severe and few insects and animals can exist.

Before a baby goat is born it is carried for five months inside its mother. Just four hours after a goat is born it is able to run and jump. They are very hairy creatures from the first day and have their eyes open.

Though people complain about some goats stinking so much, they are very useful animals. More people in the world drink goat milk than cow milk. Goat milk is often good for people with stomach trouble. Goatskins make excellent leather, and their wool is used to make good clothing.

But what makes this valuable animal such a talented climber? The heel has a soft pad on the bottom which holds to a surface like rubber. The hoof then acts like strong pincers which grab onto a rock and hold the goat steady. With these "feet," goats can climb a rock which is almost straight up and down.

It's interesting to study goats because there is so

much the average person doesn't know about them. Yet, if we are "know-it-alls" and don't listen to other people, we will never learn about the marvels of nature.

God told Job exactly the same thing about life. Job talked a lot and complained constantly but he couldn't learn anything if he refused to listen to others. God said to Job in essence, "Do you think you know everything? Then how is a goat born?" Job didn't know everything.

God wanted to tell Job about more important things than goats, but he had to be willing to listen.

We don't know everything either, and the wise person will read and listen to the Word of God.

1. Describe a goat's hoof.
2. How are goats used by man?
3. What one thing would you most like to ask God?

Do you know how mountain goats give birth? Have you ever seen them giving birth to their young? Do you know how many months of pregnancy they have before they bow themselves to give birth to their young and carry their burden no longer?—Job 39:1

forty-nine

What's So Great About Gold?

It isn't very likely that anyone would risk his life for a bucket of sand or sell all of his property so he could go and look for rocks. Yet people have done this and much more so they could find gold.

As far back as anyone can remember gold has been the most valuable mineral in the world. People are willing to pay great sums for gold for several reasons. Gold is very rare and hard to find. Gold is a very beautiful color. It is very easy to work with and can be made into bracelets, rings, and even tiny lettering. Gold lasts very well and doesn't even tarnish.

In 1848 gold was discovered in California and thousands of people rushed to the West Coast. In one year San Francisco grew by 25,000 people. Ten years later people poured into Colorado for the same reason. In 1897 Skagway, Alaska, increased by 4,000 people in just three weeks. A reported 10,000 men (prospectors) came to Alaska that year merely because they heard the word "gold."

The United States isn't the world's leading producer of gold. However, there is still a lot done here, and South Dakota has a sizable output. South Africa is the world's leader with almost twice as much gold as any other nation. While not normally thought of as a gold producer, Russia ranks as number two.

While many people work very hard to find and mine gold, a few become wealthy quite by accident. Some years ago a man was traveling by wagon in Australia when his wheel hit something in the path. When he got out to investigate he discovered a nugget of gold which weighed 208 pounds (Troy weight). Today gold is worth over $100 per ounce.

It's easy to see why people have risked their lives for gold. Many were lost in storms, starved to death and even were murdered because gold was so valuable. Yet, some people have found something worth more in life. They have read the commandments of God. They found help there, they found guidance and they found peace with God. Reading God's instructions and following them showed them the most valuable things in life.

1. When was gold discovered in California?
2. Which nation mines the most gold?
3. Name one thing more important than wealth.

While I love your commandments more than the finest gold. Every law of God is right, whatever it concerns. I hate every other way.—Psalm 119:127, 128

fifty

Candy in Israel

One day while eating a dish of ice cream I wondered what other people liked for treats. They say Eskimo children eat whale blubber for candy. But what about people of ancient Israel? They had no whales and they couldn't keep ice cream.

Children and adults enjoyed a good helping of honey for dessert. They had it all around them because bees made honey in trees, behind rocks and at least once in the bones of a dead lion. If there weren't enough bees around, mother knew a special recipe to make honey out of dates or even grapes.

It seems easy for us to buy a jar of honey, but we should remember that it took from 20,000 to 40,000 bees to prepare just one hive of honey. As the bee travels around from flower to flower, it draws some liquid (called nectar) from the blossom. The nectar is carried inside the bee's body and then deposited in the beehive. As the liquid begins to dry, it settles and becomes honey.

People in biblical times were well aware of the nutritional value of honey. It contains a form of sugar and is an excellent source of energy. It doesn't take any preparation or refinement. Honey is easy to store for long periods of time, and its great taste made it food and dessert both then and now. It wasn't uncommon for a traveler to find a honeycomb and merely help himself to a treat along the road. This is what Samson did when he returned from Timnah. He found some honey in the bones of a lion and shared it with his parents (Judges 14:8, 9).

Today we buy honey in jars at the store or when people knock on our door on Honey Bear Day to help retarded children. However, not long ago honey was sold in the very honeycomb in which the bees made it. Then one could see the many six-sided cells in which the hard working bees had placed their nectar.

For some reason vinegar has never been as popular as honey. We seldom see people put vinegar on their bread or pour a little vinegar over their cereal in the morning. The reason we don't is very obvious. Vinegar tastes bitter and honey tastes sweet and goes down a lot easier.

The person who wrote this psalm is thinking about the laws of God. Are these laws harsh and bitter and consequently hard to swallow? Or are they laws that are given because someone loves me? Are they given to help me, to protect me and give me some guidance in life?

Some people don't like any guidance or advice. They simply don't like being told what to do. They want to go out, do it their way, and no one can help them. Sometimes they get hurt a lot because they won't listen.

The psalm writer said that he needs advice and he wants it. When he reads the laws of God they are like honey. They taste good, they go down easily and they are very helpful.

1. How many bees are needed for one hive of honey?
2. Where did Samson find honey?
3. How are God's laws like honey?

No, I haven't turned away from what you taught me; your words are sweeter than honey.—Psalm 119:102, 103

fifty-one

Worship by the Seashore

Anyone who has ever gone swimming in the ocean has probably been impressed with three things about large waves: They are beautiful to see. They have a tremendous power to turn someone head over heels, and they are a lot of fun to play in.

But what is it that causes waves to rear up their heads and come crashing into the seashore? How far away do they start and what keeps them rolling?

It may come as a surprise, but when waves come rippling across a lake the water moves very little. One wave pushes another wave which pushes a third wave. It is not a case of thirty big waves rolling for thirty miles. Rather water pushes water which pushes water.

This can be most clearly seen when one drops a rock into still water. One ripple pushes another ripple which pushes a third. Consequently, when waves beat against a rock it is essentially the same water hitting the rock time after time.

The ripple of a wave may start many miles away. A summer wave hitting the coast of California may have started 6,000 miles away at New Zealand. The steady wind keeps the waves rolling all the way across the ocean.

If the water is moved by a hurricane, the waves may reach higher than a house. One ship measured and reported that it was hit by a wave 112 feet high.

The power behind large waves is enormous. At Tillamook Rock, Oregon, a wave hit the shore with such force it sent a 135-pound rock flying into the air and smashed it into a house.

In some circumstances waves can be dangerous for swimmers. If conditions are right and the swimmer is not careful, he can be literally pulled out miles to sea. However, usually a lifeguard will close down a beach if such waves are present.

A lot of people joke about worshipping God out in nature among the stars and forest. However, many ancient believers did not consider it strange. They could worship God in temples or churches, but other times their hearts filled with appreciation merely by walking along the beach.

The next time we see the splendor of a wave cracking against a rocky shore, we might want to pause and think about God. His strength, His majesty, His creation, His supply of water, His gift of recreation, and so much more. Nature isn't the only place we find God, but He is certainly there.

1. How do waves move across the ocean?
2. Describe the power of waves.
3. What do you consider to be some of God's greatest creations?

Jehovah is King! He is robed in majesty and strength. The world is his throne.
O Lord, you have reigned from prehistoric times, from the everlasting past. The mighty oceans thunder your praise. You are mightier than all the breakers pounding on the seashores of the world. — Psalm 93:1-4

fifty-two

Does He Care About Hair?

Have you ever heard a story of someone who was frightened so badly that his hair turned white? There are a lot of stories that get passed around like this, but they probably aren't very accurate. Each hair on our head comes out of an individual root, and in order for it to become gray the hair has to turn color down by the scalp and then grow out.

Hair is a very important part of the body, but it is more important for animals than for people. Some animals have their bodies covered with hair for protection. Other animals have very little hair and are protected by thick skin. People don't have thick enough skin or enough hair so they need to wear clothes.

For most people their hair grows at a rate of about three-quarters of an inch each month. Hair grows faster at night than in the day and faster in the summer than winter.

Many people have guessed as to why some hair is curly and other is straight. They have wondered if the weather or wearing a hat makes someone's hair curly. Actually the sole determining factor is in the shape of the root. If our hair roots are round, our hair will grow straight. If the roots are flat, the hair will be curly.

Some people begin to lose their hair as they grow older and may become bald. This usually means that something has happened to the roots. So far there seems to be no cure for baldness. Very often baldness depends on whether or not our parents are bald, and this is called heredity.

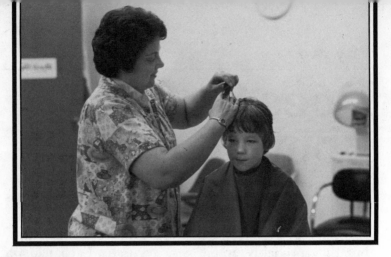

It hurts to have our hair pulled, but there is no feeling when it is cut. This is because there are no nerves in our hair, but if it is pulled there is pressure on the roots and the roots have nerves.

Though hair has an importance, it is hardly the most important part of our body. Every day we throw away hair that we pull out of our comb or we can see loose hairs which have fallen on our sweater. To lose a few pieces here and there doesn't mean much to most of us. And yet to God every hair has significance, and at any moment He knows just how many are on your head and mine.

Not that God spends each day with a pocket calculator counting hair. He doesn't need to count, He just knows. That shows a tremendous personal interest in each one of us.

1. When does hair grow the fastest?
2. Why doesn't your hair hurt when it's cut?
3. What do you think God is like?

Not one sparrow (What do they cost? Two for a penny?) can fall to the ground without your Father knowing it. And the very hairs of your head are all numbered. — Matthew 10:29, 30.